THINGS ARE MADE to MOVE

By Illa Podendorf

Illustrations by Jane Ike

 CHILDRENS PRESS, CHICAGO

Illa Podendorf, former chairman of the Science Department of the Laboratory Schools, University of Chicago, has prepared this series of books with emphasis on the processes of science. The content is selected from the main branches of science—biology, physics, and chemistry—but the thrust is on the process skills which are essential in scientific work. Some of the processes emphasized are observing, classifying, communicating, measuring, inferring, and predicting. The treatment is intellectually stimulating which makes it occupy an active part in a child's thinking. This is important in all general education of children.

This book, *Things Are Made to Move,* provides opportunities for observing the movement in a variety of common objects. References are made to inferences based upon observations which are made.

Library of Congress Catalog Card Number: 75-123799

3 4 5 6 7 8 9 10 11 12 13 14 15 16 17 18 19 20 21 22 23 24 25 R 75 74

CONTENTS

WE PLAY WITH THINGS THAT MOVE

Mary has a toy that moves.
She turns a key.
She puts the toy on the floor.
It moves.

Jane has a toy that moves.
Jane pushes something.
She puts the toy on the floor.
It moves.

Bob has a truck that will move
across the floor.
First Bob must wind it up tight.
Then the truck will move.

Charles has a train.
He turns it on. It runs around
the track.

The jack-in-the-box jumps up
when the lid is opened

Here are more toys that move.
What must be done to them to
make them move?

You can INFER from what you see
what must be done.

You can see keys.
They need to be wound up.

Mary's toy, Bob's truck, the
jack-in-the-box, and all the toys
on page 11 are alike in one way.
They all have a special part
that makes them move.
You cannot see it in the pictures.

Do you have an idea of what
it is?

You can only infer what it is.
If you could see it, you would
know it is a kind of spring.

This spring looks
like this when it is
wound up tight.

This spring is not
wound up tight.

The jack-in-the-box
spring looks like this when
the lid of the box
is closed.

Jane's duck and Charles's train
move.

But it is not a spring that
makes them move.

Can you infer what it is?

Look closely at the pictures on
pages 6 and 8. You may see
something that makes you feel sure
that what you inferred is right.

Did you infer that electricity
makes those toys move?

It does.

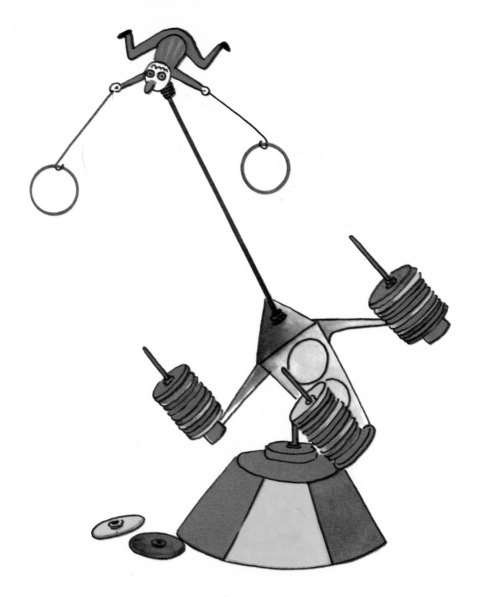

The round weights keep this
little fellow swinging in the air.
When some of the round weights are
moved he may go toppling.

Something makes all of these
things work.

The clown moves when it is tipped,
because of the weights in it.

Can you infer, from what you can
see, which toys have a spring?
Only one does not.

Mark and John played on a teeter-totter.

They knew it would work only if they sat in certain places.

The teeter-totter is something like which toys you have seen in this book?

Did you look on page 15?

These boys are learning to ski.
The snow is very smooth. They
go downhill fast on their skis.

These girls are having fun on a
sled.

How is being on a sled like
being on skis?

WE RIDE ON THINGS
THAT MOVE

We ride on ships.
We ride on sailboats.

We ride in buses.
We ride in cars.

We ride on planes.
We ride on trains.

Sailboats, ships, buses, cars, planes, and trains all need something to keep them going.

One needs something quite different than the others.

Can you decide which one that is? Did you think of the sailboat?

OTHER THINGS
CAN MAKE THINGS MOVE

Water makes things move.
Water turns this wheel.
A waterwheel causes other wheels
to turn and work for us.

Water can move many things. Is it moving more than one thing in this picture?

Something is making the hat,
the umbrella, the leaves, and the
papers move. Can you infer what it is?
What else is the wind moving?

The rope on a pulley can be made
to lift a heavy bucket.

Rocks roll downhill.
Do you think their
weight and where they
were has anything to
do with their rolling
downhill?

Can you make
an inference
about what started
them rolling?

Could it have been this,

or the water,

or this?

Apples fall from trees.
What can you infer about
these apples?

Did you infer that they are
ripe and heavy?
Did you infer that the wind
blew them off?
Either inference is a good one.

Something in thermometers moves.

Some thermometers have alcohol in them.

Some have mercury.

It is the alcohol or mercury that moves up and down.

Notice the two thermometers.

One is the Fahrenheit scale. The other is the Celsius scale.

The Fahrenheit scale says the temperature is 86 degrees. The Celsius scale says that the temperature is 30 degrees.

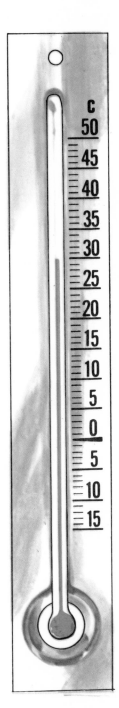
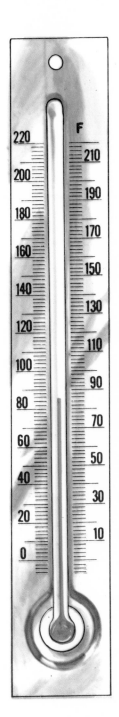

Here are two thermometers.

In warm sunshine.

In a cool place.

You may infer from looking at the two thermometers that alcohol or mercury expands and moves up when it is heated.

You might also infer that the alcohol or mercury will contract and move down when it is cooled.

Your inferences are good ones.

Your body temperature, when you are well, is 98.6 degrees Fahrenheit.

What is it on the Celsius reading?

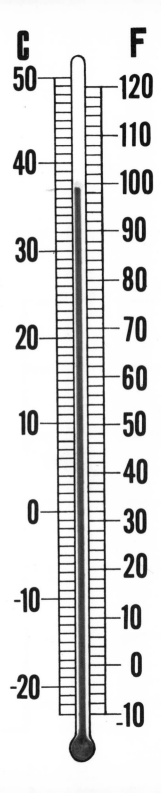

WE MAKE THINGS MOVE

What can you infer from this picture?

You are almost sure to infer that Jim made the bat move, and the bat made the ball move.

Jim is making more than one
thing move in this picture.
How many inferences can you make
about what they might be?

Find something which you think
is being moved in each of these pictures.

WE MOVE

Johnny has been running.
He is so tired he thinks he
cannot move.

His mother gave him his supper.
Then he went to bed. He slept.

The next morning he ate his breakfast. He was ready to go again.

Food and rest gave Johnny his energy.

We could not run, jump, climb,
or swim if we did not have food
and enough rest.

Boys could not play ball if
they did not have food and rest.

We could not climb trees, mow the lawn, or do homework without food and rest to give us energy.

All animals need food and rest so that they can move.

People and animals
move and
make other things move.

They get their energy from food
and rest.

NOW WE KNOW

Things would not move if there was no energy.

It may come from a wound-up spring.

It may come from electricity.

It may come from position.

It may come from fuel like gasoline, oil, or coal.

It may come from the heat of the sun.

It may come from running water, or from wind.

It may come from food we eat.